Little Secrets of Friendship

*They'll dazzle your heart
each day of the month*

J. Donald Walters

Hardbound edition, first printing 1994

Copyright 1994
J. Donald Walters

Text illustrations: Karen White
Cover design: Sara Cryer

Illustrations Copyright 1994
Crystal Clarity, Publishers

ISBN 1-56589-602-5

10 9 8 7 6 5 4 3 2

PRINTED IN HONG KONG

Crystal Clarity
P U B L I S H E R S

14618 Tyler Foote Road, Nevada City, CA 95959
1 (800) 424-1055

Keep one page open

each day.

Think of the secret on that page.

Feel what it says.

Hold it inside your heart so deeply

you'll find golden dreams awaiting you

in sleep.

Every morning,

when you awake,

a new, secret friend

will be there,

smiling within you.

Day 1

Choose friends who are sincere with you, not those who only make you feel important. If your jacket billows in the wind, you may look bigger in it, but it won't keep you warm.

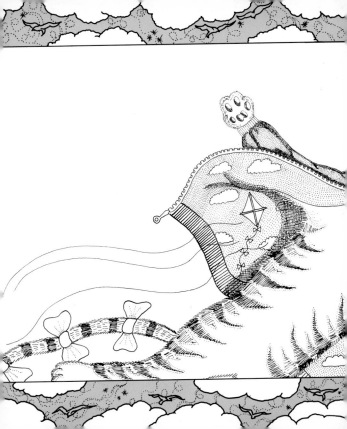

Day 2

Understand that you must *be* a friend to others, first. For friendship, like a silver cup, grows dull if you leave it uncared for, shines if you polish it, and shines brightest of all if you focus light on it.

Day 3

Give your friends freedom to be themselves.
Choose friends, too, who will give you that
same freedom. Isn't life more interesting for
its differences? The canary can't fly as
fast as the hummingbird, but
it sings beautifully.
The hummingbird,
though it flies fast,
can't sing at all.

Day 4

Expand your happiness by sharing it with others. The larger a rainbow, the more brightly it shines.

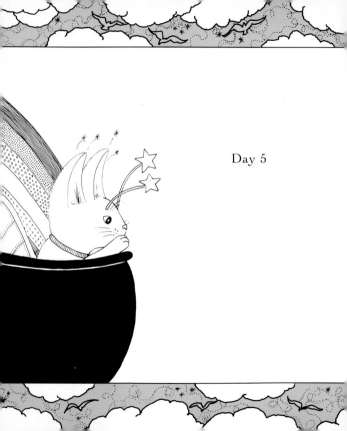

Day 5

Listen more, and talk less. Let your friends tell you how *they* feel about things. Who likes a dog that does nothing but bark?

Don't only *talk* friendship: *Be* a friend. *Show* your friendship by the things you do for others. Don't be a talking parrot, which can be taught to say, "I like you," but will never understand what those words mean.

Day 6

Day 7

Like people. Don't measure their words to see how well they like you. A fire in the fireplace is there to provide warmth, not to be warmed. If you warm others by your friendship, they will always crowd around you.

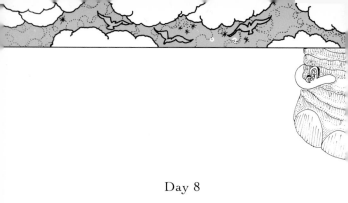

Day 8

When you appreciate what your friends say or do, *show* them your appreciation. Don't take it for granted that they recognize it. Don't we all feel more friendly toward a dog when it wags its tail?

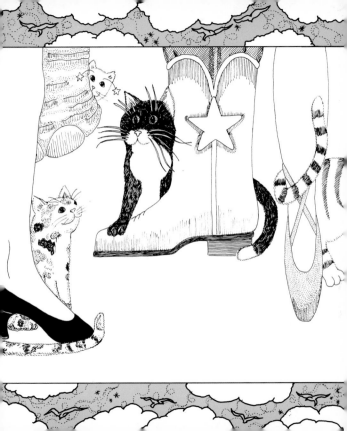

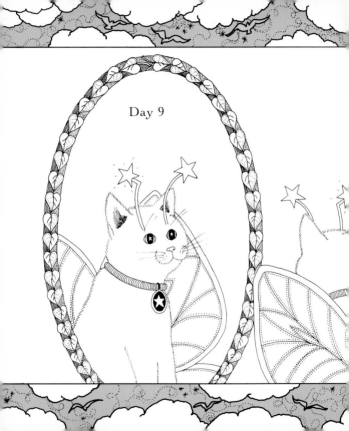

Day 9

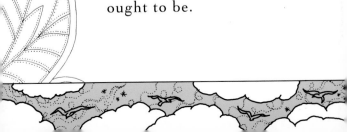

Accept your friends as they are, and they'll accept you as you are. If you think friendship should be perfect, look at yourself sometime in the mirror. Are *you* perfect? By accepting what *is*, we can all grow together toward what ought to be.

Day 10

Don't give your bad moods to others. That's like giving them a wormy apple to eat.

Day 11

Make your friends' needs as important as your own. Nobody likes a person who always shoves his way to the front of a line.

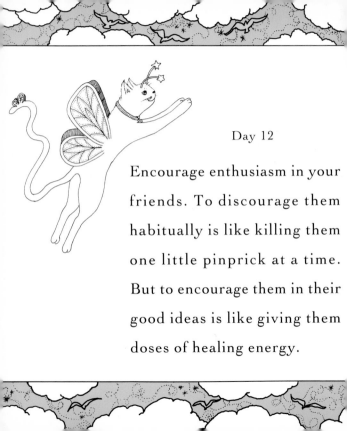

Day 12

Encourage enthusiasm in your friends. To discourage them habitually is like killing them one little pinprick at a time. But to encourage them in their good ideas is like giving them doses of healing energy.

Day 13

Let others have their say, even if you disagree with them. Once you've heard them out, then tell them, kindly but truthfully, what *you* think.

Day 14

Don't mix with people for what you hope to get out of them. Mix with them for themselves. *Like* them for themselves. Nobody wants to hang around with pickpockets.

Day 15

Express your feelings through your eyes. Don't be so wrapped up in yourself that people have to shake you, like a Christmas present, to guess what's inside.

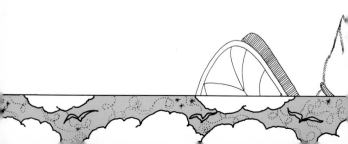

Express your friendship through the tone of your voice. A warm voice says, "I like you," better than words ever can.

Day 17

Don't only *play* with your friends. Be serious with them, too. Discuss with them what you think about things, and about life. Talk about what you hope to do with your lives. Don't let your play become like the wind-scattered leaves, torn away from the tree that kept them green.

When you're with friends, *be* with them wholeheartedly. Don't let your eyes go roaming about while you think of other things. A sputtering candle gives only feeble light. Even so, a person who pays only careless attention to his friends will create only feeble friendships.

Don't let disagreements affect your friendship for others. Be true to them, no matter what. If they speak unkindly to you, be like a flowering cherry tree: Each time they strike you, shower them with blossoms of your kindness.

Day 19

Day 20

Concentrate on the things you like about your friends, and overlook what you don't like. The notes one plays on a piano are the notes that get sounded.

Try not to criticize others. Instead, make helpful suggestions. The way to be happy yourself is to make others happy. And the surest way to be unhappy yourself is to make others unhappy. The color you paint a fence is the color you get on your clothes.

Day 21

Day 22

Don't be a part-time friend. Even if a friend turns away from you, support him silently. Be like a star, shining steadily no matter how dark the night.

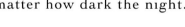

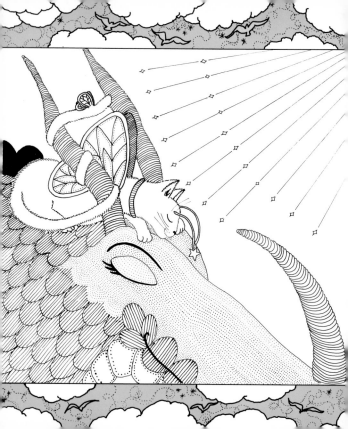

Day 23

Be faithful to what is true and good in your friends, but don't encourage them in their weaknesses. Be like the sunlight: Offer life and healing to all.

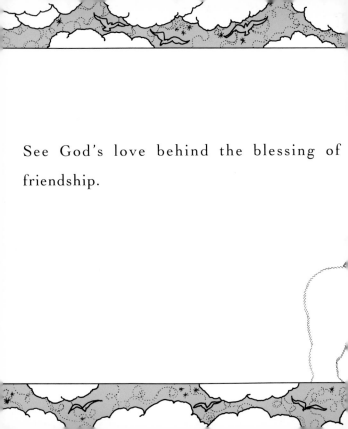

See God's love behind the blessing of friendship.

Day 24

Day 25

Be true to your word, and to the promises you make. Be like a strong tree to which people cling when a river is in flood.

Day 26

Look for things you can learn from your friends. Think of your times together as times to grow in understanding. The wolf cub plays at hunting so that, later on, the wolf may be a good hunter.

Day 27

Live by truth as you best understand it. Your friends will respect you if you stand straight, like a fir tree, while others bend like meadow grass before every breeze.

Day 28

Give your friends one of life's most precious gifts: respect. When laughing together, laugh *at* them only if you can laugh just as happily when they laugh at you. Wavelets on a lake play together in the breeze. Be a wise wavelet, never forgetting that you and your wavelet friends are all part of the same body of water.

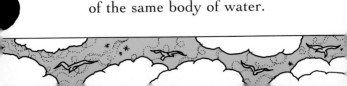

Day 29

See God as your truest friend of all.

Day 30

In your loyalty to others, be like the oak tree, which, though buffeted by winds, never ceases to offer people shade.

Day 31

Don't try to be like anyone else: Be yourself.
There isn't any "best" way to be. An elephant
isn't "better" than a cat. If you're an
elephant, be a good elephant. If you're a cat,
be the best cat you know how to be.

Other Books in the **Secrets** Series
by J. Donald Walters

Little Secrets of Success

Little Secrets of Happiness

Life's Little Secrets

Secrets of Love

Secrets of Happiness

Secrets of Friendship

Secrets of Inner Peace

Secrets of Success

Secrets for Men

Secrets for Women

Secrets of Prosperity

Secrets of Self-Acceptance

Secrets of Winning People

Secrets of Bringing Peace on Earth

Secrets of Leadership

Selected Other Titles
by J. Donald Walters

Education for Life - views all life as a school, and gives insights into our stages of growth and understanding.

The Path - the autobiography of J. Donald Walters.

Audio

All the World Is My Friend - children's music composed by J. Donald Walters and performed by children.

If you cannot find these titles at your local gift or bookstore, write or call: Crystal Clarity, Publishers, 14618 Tyler Foote Road, Nevada City, CA 95959, or call 1-800-424-1055.

℺